Theory Paper Grade 4   2013   A
Model Answers

CW00386403

1 (a) slow   (2)
            sad   (2)
     (b) submediant   (2)
     (c) A♭ major   (2)
     (d) 24   (2)
     (e)   (2)

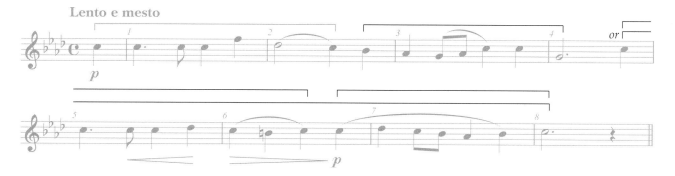

     (f)   (3)

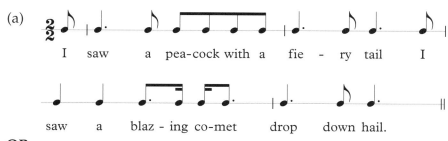

2 *There are many ways of completing this question. Either of the specimen completions below would receive full marks.* (10)

EITHER

(a)

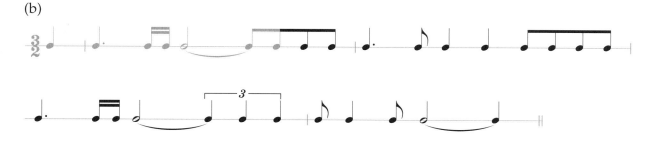

OR

(b)

3

3 (a) (i) animated enough / lively enough / sufficiently animated / sufficiently lively (4)

(ii) acciaccatura / grace note / crushed note (2)

(iii) 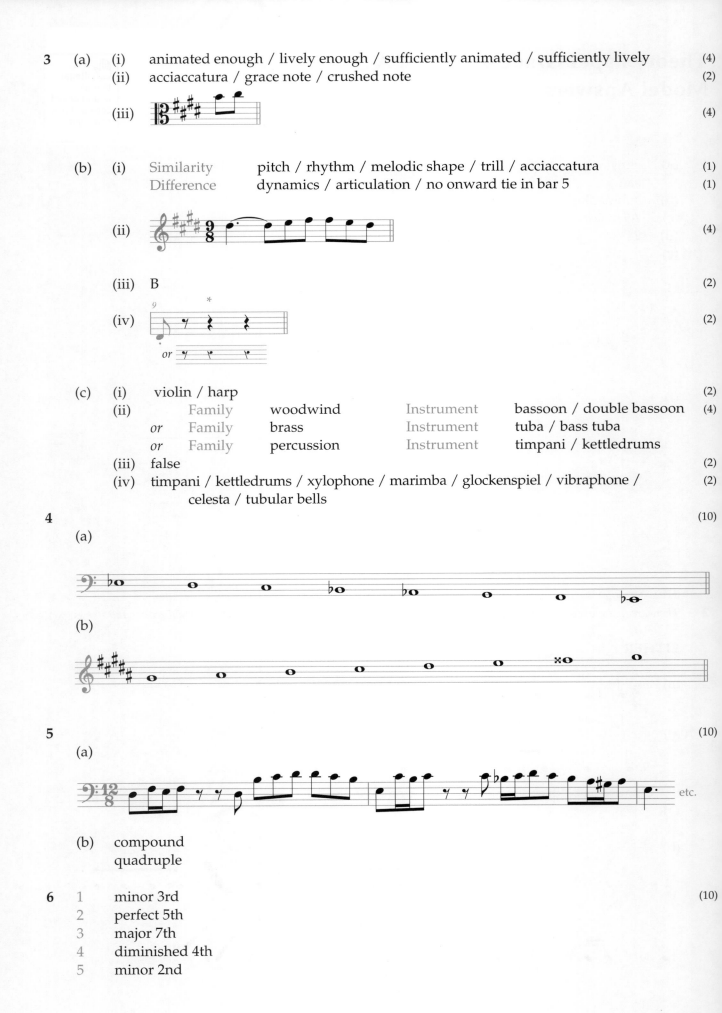 (4)

(b) (i) Similarity — pitch / rhythm / melodic shape / trill / acciaccatura (1)

Difference — dynamics / articulation / no onward tie in bar 5 (1)

(ii) (4)

(iii) B (2)

(iv) (2)

or

(c) (i) violin / harp (2)

(ii)   Family   woodwind   Instrument   bassoon / double bassoon (4)
or Family   brass   Instrument   tuba / bass tuba
or Family   percussion   Instrument   timpani / kettledrums

(iii) false (2)

(iv) timpani / kettledrums / xylophone / marimba / glockenspiel / vibraphone / celesta / tubular bells (2)

4 (10)

(a)

(b)

5 (10)

(a)

(b) compound
quadruple

6 1 minor 3rd (10)
2 perfect 5th
3 major 7th
4 diminished 4th
5 minor 2nd

7 (a) (1) tonic / I   (9)
         (2) subdominant / IV
         (3) dominant / V

(b)    (6)

Theory Paper Grade 4   2013   B
Model Answers

1 (a) as if / resembling / like   (2)
         slightly faster than walking pace / slightly slower than walking pace /   (2)
            slightly faster than medium speed / slightly slower than medium speed

(b) [musical notation]   (4)

(c) two / two semiquavers / two 16th notes / one quaver / one eighth note   (2)
(d) six   (2)
(e) semiquaver / 16th note   (1)
(f) Similarity   melodic shape / rhythm / both *p*   (1)
     Difference   pitch   (1)

2 *There are many ways of completing this question. Either of the specimen completions below would receive full marks.*   (10)

EITHER

(a)

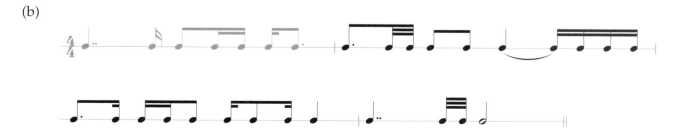

OR

(b)

5

3 **(a)** **(i)** getting a little louder / getting a bit louder / getting slightly louder / (2)
gradually getting a little louder / gradually getting a bit louder /
gradually getting slightly louder

(ii) *animato*   *vivace*   (4)

(iii) simple   (1)
triple   (1)

(iv) 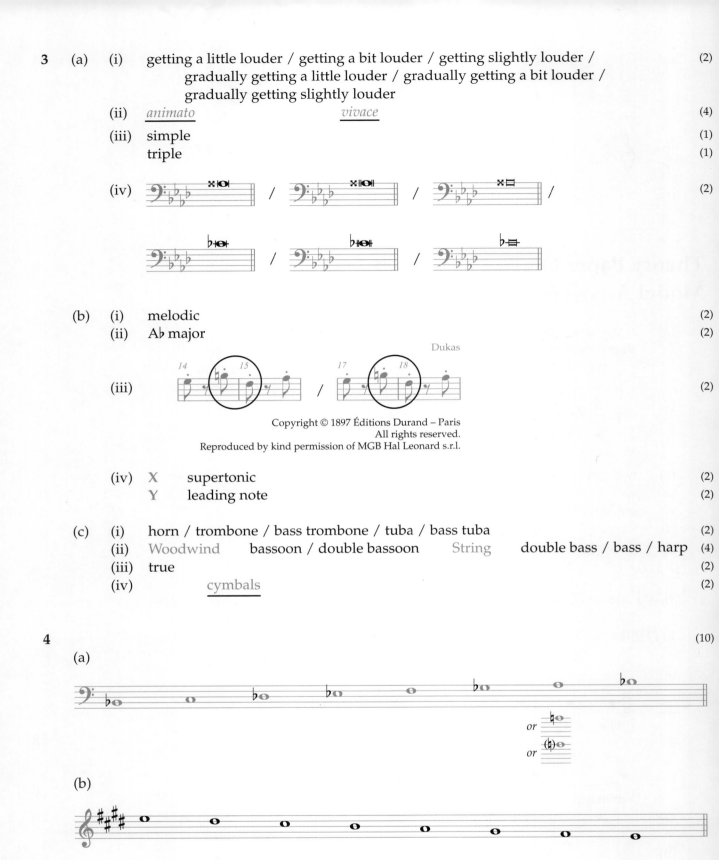   (2)

(b) **(i)** melodic   (2)
(ii) A♭ major   (2)

(iii)   (2)

(iv) X   supertonic   (2)
Y   leading note   (2)

(c) **(i)** horn / trombone / bass trombone / tuba / bass tuba   (2)
(ii) Woodwind   bassoon / double bassoon   String   double bass / bass / harp   (4)
(iii) true   (2)
(iv)   cymbals   (2)

4   (10)

(a)

(b)

5 (10)

6   A flat   E double sharp   (10)
     F flat   C sharp
     C double flat   G / G natural

7   (a)   (1)   tonic / I   (9)
            (2)   dominant / V
            (3)   subdominant / IV

     (b)   G minor   B minor   E major   (6)
           dominant / V   subdominant / IV   tonic / I

Theory Paper Grade 4   2013   C
Model Answers

1   (a)      (2)

     (b)   slow enough / sufficiently slow   (4)
     (c)   B♭ minor   (2)
     (d)   A♭   (2)
     (e)      (2)

     (f)   (2)

     (g)   true   (1)

2 *There are many ways of completing this question. Either of the specimen completions below would receive full marks.* (10)

EITHER

(a)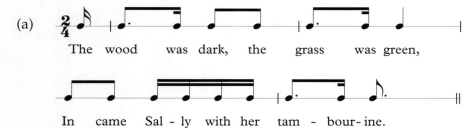

The wood   was dark,   the   grass   was green,

In   came   Sal – ly   with her   tam – bour- ine.

OR

(b)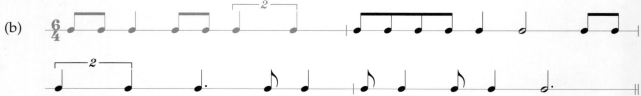

3 (a) (i) broadly (2)
           expressive / expressively / with expression (2)
       (ii) acciaccatura / grace note / crushed note (2)
       (iii) compound (1)
           quadruple (1)
       (iv) 22 (2)

   (b) (i) X   mediant (2)
           Y   dominant (2)

       (ii) (4)

       (iii) three / three quavers / three eighth notes / one dotted crotchet / one dotted (2)
           quarter note / one beat

   (c) (i) violin / harp (2)
       (ii) Highest   trumpet (2)
           Lowest   tuba / bass tuba (2)
       (iii) false (2)
           true (2)

4 (10)

(a)

(b)

5  (10)

6 1   augmented 2nd   (10)
   2   major 3rd
   3   diminished 5th
   4   perfect 4th
   5   minor 6th

7 (a)   (1)   subdominant / IV   (9)
       (2)   dominant / V
       (3)   tonic / I

   (b)       (6)

Theory Paper Grade 4   2013   S
Model Answers

1 (a)   76 crotchets in a minute / 76 quarter notes in a minute / 76 crotchet beats in a minute /   (2)
          76 quarter-note beats in a minute
       prominent / make the melody stand out   (2)
       getting quieter / gradually getting quieter   (1)

   (b)   (4)

   (c)   *There are five possible answers to this question. Any of the answers shown would receive full marks.*   (2)

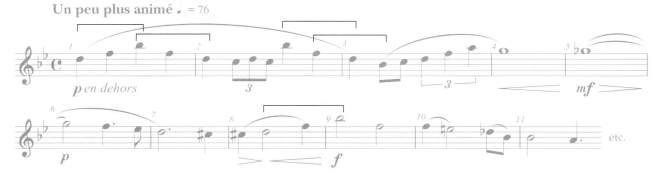

(d) *All possible answers are shown on the extract reproduced below. For full marks candidates need to identify*   (2)
    only two of the answers, each with a different letter name.

(e) two / two crotchets / two quarter notes / one minim / one half note   (2)

2 *There are many ways of completing this question. Either of the specimen completions below would receive full marks.*   (10)

EITHER

(a)
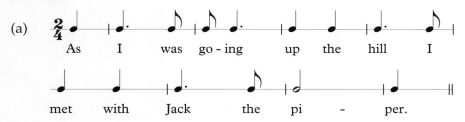

OR

(b)

3 (a) (i)   nobly   (2)
                 on the G string   (2)
             (ii) trill / shake   (2)
             (iii) major 6th   (2)
             (iv) two   (2)

     (b) (i)   flute / oboe / clarinet   (2)
             (ii) String   cello / double bass /   Brass   trombone / bass trombone /   (4)
                              bass / harp   tuba / bass tuba
             (iii) violin   viola   (4)

     (c) (i)   Similarity   rhythm / melodic shape / articulation   (1)
                 Difference   pitch / dynamics   (1)
             (ii) mediant   (2)

             (iii)   (4)

(iv) 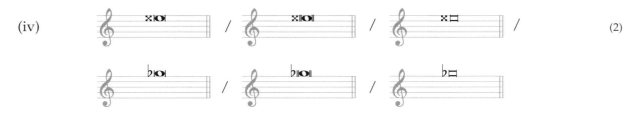　(2)

4　(10)

(a)

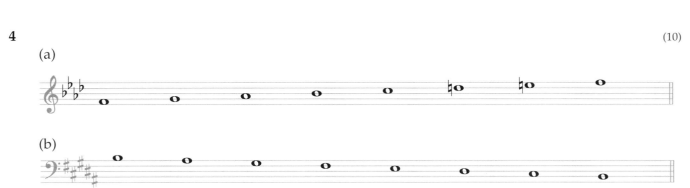

(b)

5　(10)

(a)

(b)

6　(10)

7　(a)　(1)　dominant / V　(9)
　　　　(2)　tonic / I
　　　　(3)　subdominant / IV

(b)　　　　　　　　　　　　　　　　　　　　　(6)

Music Theory Past Papers 2013 Model Answers

Model answers for four past papers from ABRSM's 2013 Theory exams for Grade 4

Key features:

- a list of correct answers where appropriate
- a selection of likely options where the answer can be expressed in a variety of ways
- a single exemplar where a composition-style answer is required

Support material for ABRSM Theory exams

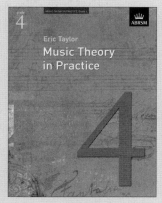

ABRSM
24 Portland Place
London W1B 1LU
United Kingdom

www.abrsm.org

ABRSM is the exam board of the Royal Schools of Music. We are committed to actively supporting high-quality music-making, learning and development throughout the world, and to producing the best possible resources for music teachers and students.

ISBN 978-1-84849-617-0

£3·50

Music Theory
Past Papers
2013
Model Answers

ABRSM Grade 4

Welcome to ABRSM's *Music Theory Past Papers 2013 Model Answers*, Grade 4. These answers are a useful resource for students and teachers preparing for ABRSM theory exams and should be used alongside the relevant published theory past papers.

All the answers in this booklet would receive full marks but not all possible answers have been included for practicable reasons. In these cases other reasonable alternatives may also be awarded full marks. For composition-style questions (where candidates must complete a rhythm, compose a melody based on a given opening or set text to music) only one example of the many possible answers is given.

For more information on how theory papers are marked and some general advice on taking theory exams, please refer to the Music Theory Grade 4 web page: www.abrsm.org/theory4.

Using these answers

- Answers are given in the same order and, where possible, in the same layout as in the exam papers, making it easy to match answer to question.

- Where it is necessary to show the answer on a stave, the original stave is printed in grey with the answer shown in black, for example:

- Alternative answers are separated by an oblique stroke (/) or by *or*, for example:

getting slower / gradually getting slower

- Answers that require the candidate to write out a scale or chord have been shown at one octave only. Reasonable alternatives at different octaves can also receive full marks.

© 2014 by The Associated Board of the Royal Schools of Music
Published by ABRSM (Publishing) Ltd, a wholly owned subsidiary of ABRSM
Cover by Kate Benjamin & Andy Potts
Printed in England by Page Bros (Norwich) Ltd
Reprinted in 2015